Living the Full Life
Devotions on Aging

Donald R. Jarman, D. Min

LUCAS
PARK
BOOKS

ST. LOUIS, MISSOURI

ISBN: 978-1-60350-068-5

Published by Lucas Park books www.lucasparkbooks.com

Printed in the United States of America

Contents

You're Not Finished

For almost five years I conducted devotions and communion at a retirement community in Beaverton, Oregon. On the second Sunday of each month, musicians from Murray Hills Christian Church (Disciples of Christ) joined me in a service. Some Sundays the attendance was commendable, some Sundays it was only "when two or three are gathered together." Attendance, in fact, fluctuated with the yearly change in fees and changes in need at the retirement community. I was often told I was the only ordained minister who brought a service and the only one who offered communion. The other services during the month were conducted by a number of local congregations and loyal laypersons. Of course, being Christian Church (Disciples of Christ), our tradition is to participate in The Lord's Supper and gather at The Table on the first day of the week.

It was challenging. I sought to deliver a message to older adults that supported their faith. I did what I could to inspire moving beyond a "Come to Jesus" message. The title of this book, *Living the Full Life*, was inspired by hearing the bereaved at funerals I conducted say about their lost loved one, "Mother (or Dad) lived a full life." I often wondered just what that meant and decided to dedicate my book to the idea of living a full life and the reality that even in aging one is not finished living.

Finally, I make no claims to being a scholar, even though I have both a Masters of Divinity and a Doctor of Ministry from highly accredited seminaries and studied under prominent scholars of theology. I have been a local pastor, a crisis counselor in a hospital, a director of development and fundraiser, and a project manager on both church buildings and retirement facilities. And I have taught throughout the Pacific Northwest on the concerns of the elderly. Now in my senior years I wish to publish the meditations of my heart and faith regarding aging.

My heart-felt appreciation goes to Sharon Jarman, M.A., who has encouraged me, and done a little nagging; my son Mark Jarman, Centennial Professor of English at Vanderbilt University, my initial reviewer; my late sister, Mary Ellen Elliott, in her advanced years, was an astute and voluminous reader who counseled me to *"just do it!"*; all those professors in college, seminary, and graduate school who put up with me, taught me and opened my eyes to the wonders and strength of faith; and my current pastor who, though at times we are at odds, has still helped me to be a person in the pew listening and learning. There are also many who listened to me as I preached, taught, told stories, and said, "You ought to write a book." Here it is.

How to Use This Book

This is a devotional book. It is neither a book of fiction nor is it a text book. Its purpose is to be read for devotion and also, if you wish, use it as a guide for prayer.

When I was a young minister and pastoring my first church full time I met up with an older adult woman who lived a block from the church. She was a devout Methodist and also a member of a pioneer family in Santa Maria, CA. I don't quite remember how our paths crossed other than she took a liking to me and became my champion. On Sundays she attended both my service and the service at the First Methodist Church.

When I first went into her house, I noticed a large yellow legal pad on her dining room table. A closer look revealed it contained a list of names and she told me it was her "work". I then learned that every hour she would sit down at the table and go over the names expressing a prayer for each name. That was her work.

In this book you will find at the close of each chapter a blank page. At the top of the page will be a two to three line prayer. You are encouraged to turn to that page, after reading the scripture and devotion, and have a personal private prayer. You may use the blank page to write names, joys and concerns influenced by your devotions.

This book is meant for your use, personally and prayerfully.

Where Faith Begins

And passing along the Sea of Galilee, he saw Simon
and Andrew the brother of Simon casting a net in
the sea; for they were fishermen. And Jesus said to
them, "Follow me and I will make you become fishers
of men." And immediately they left their nets and
followed him.

Mark 1: 16 – 18

In the history of the denomination in which I was raised,
and later a pastor, we had "the five finger exercise." It was
a teaching mechanism to instruct potential converts to the
Restoration Movement, that is, The Christian Church (Disciples
of Christ). The five fingers are Faith, Repentance, Baptism,
Forgiveness, and The Holy Spirit. Note that this is an outline of
the basic belief, not a creed, nor a complicated doctrine, nor a
dogma to which you must adhere. It begins with faith, and that
faith is self-determined.

Where do you start?

You may be just starting to search your faith; you may have
a history similar to mine; you may have made your commitment
in a different denomination. We have a variety of backgrounds
and beginnings. I am willing to guess we have been influenced
by the manner in which we were raised and taught by parents,
grandparents, teachers, and ministers.

Once, a young man with a strong religious background
invaded my art class. I was painting a narrative picture of an
incident depicted in one of my son's poems. It was a story of my
being called out in the night to a home where a teenage girl had
shot herself. The young man stood at my easel and asked what
I was painting. When I told him he announced with emphatic
authority that the girl had gone to hell. I responded that I was

4

in no position to judge such a tragedy, not having all the facts. He then responded that his mother was a true believer in the Bible and this was what she had taught him. So many of us believe loyally what we have learned "at Mother's knee" and struggle as we get older with new knowledge and new insight. Our understanding of God is all too often influenced by all sorts of images, ideals, fantasies, and symbols. The great painter Michelangelo has greatly influenced our image of God, whether we have seen his painting in the Sistine Chapel or not. His depiction of God creating Adam on the Sistine Chapel's ceiling is overwhelming. There God is among the clouds, massive, bearded, reaching out to give Adam life. And so we think of God ever since as a bearded superman in the heavens creating our life.

But then we are confronted with the scripture that says, "God is spirit, and those who worship him must worship in spirit and truth." (John 4: 24) And we go, "Duh!"

Read the book of Mark. It will take about the same amount of time it takes to read the morning paper. You will find a concise, uncomplicated story of the life of Jesus. It skips much of what we have gathered into our faith system; it is simple and direct and probably the first book written about Jesus's life. In this time in which we live there is so much clutter in our lives. We are inundated with the subjective thinking of so many people and thrown into the experience of what is called reality by the TV and other influences. Stop and just read Mark, read it again, and then contemplate what you have been told, experienced, and read. Don't be afraid to ask questions and even question what you have seen and heard. Know that your insight will change as you learn. What is most important is that in this process you have the freedom to search and be free of what we call "the test of faith." The young man standing at my easel believed in a test; he gave me a test even as he had been tested many times by his loyalty to his mother's teachings. He would not have asked if he had not been uncertain, for in his college experience he was being exposed to all sorts of new ideas and he was having his own trouble organizing them and being loyal to what his mother said and to the judgment that he thought might come down upon him if he dared to question.

Yes, it is difficult to come to an individual awareness, to reach into what may be an unknown and find an understanding completely contrary to what has been instilled in you from some other source.

There is a significant fact about the author of Mark. He does take some things for granted. He does not need supernatural phenomena to convince him of what he is telling. He does not necessarily make an argument for the existence of God. He believes and he tells about Jesus performing miracles. Mark is a story about trust, belief, and faith. People who need help come to Jesus out of trust and belief. Jesus teaches his disciples about trust and belief. Dig a little deeper in Mark.

Do you understand the idea of matter? All around us are examples of matter, form, substance, even our bodies are examples of matter. But in a higher form we have life. A rock can be matter but a higher level is life – matter that is living, the trees, the animals, and ourselves.

And yet we look at ourselves and we often say we have mind. I walk my dogs and wonder, "What are they thinking? Do they have a mind?" Sometimes when I give them a command I wonder if they have any understanding as they look at me. But I can teach them by rote to sit, stay, fetch. All I have to do is take their halters off the hook and they are ready to go for a walk. And yet I do know that though they may have something called a mind, they do not have a soul. You and I who are of an even higher form do have a soul. Sometimes we do wonder about the soul that occupies a mind, when we see certain things happening not only in our lives but in others. We have come to believe that the soul determines our actions, our understanding and compassion.

The next level is a complete consciousness and we call it spirit. Jesus told the woman at the well in John 4: 24, "God is spirit." To understand the worship which we do is to understand that God is spirit. This is the ultimate truth and higher than matter, life, mind, or soul. We can live with this and grow in our understanding and know that life is a never ending process and constant growth.

I believe I have experienced in the New Testament Church the desire to reach a higher level of awareness. The key is the person and work of the Jesus of history. Living as he did Jesus became the consummate revelation of what his forebears were telling in the ages before him. They grew in awareness of the reality of spirit and the reality of love.

"By this all will know that you are my disciples, if you have love for one another." (John 13: 35) The world will come to believe us not by the practice of dogma but by the visibility of our love. We believe in the revelation of the ultimate, a spirit that is the foundation of our faith. And this foundation in history has been revealed to us in the person and work of Jesus the Christ.

Our creator,
establish for me beginnings,
so in my life I can celebrate your love.

A Part of Something Grand

1 Remember also your Creator in the days of your youth, before the evil days come, and the years draw nigh, when you will say, "I have no pleasure in them"; 2 before the sun and the light and the moon and the stars are darkened and the clouds return after the rain; 3 in the day when the keepers of the house tremble, and the strong men are bent, and the grinders cease because they are few, and those that look through the windows are dimmed, 4 and the doors on the street are shut; when the sound of the grinding is low, and one rises up at the voice of a bird, and all the daughters of song are brought low; 5 they are afraid also of what is high, and terrors are in the way; the almond tree blossoms, the grasshopper drags itself along and desire fails; because man goes to his eternal home, and the mourners go about the streets; 6 before the silver cord is snapped, or the golden bowl is broken, or the pitcher is broken at the fountain, or the wheel broken at the cistern, 7 and the dust returns to the earth as it was, and the spirit returns to God who gave it. 8 Vanity of vanities, says the Preacher; all is vanity.

9 Besides being wise, the Preacher also taught the people knowledge, weighing and studying and arranging proverbs with great care. 10 The Preacher sought to find pleasing words, and uprightly he wrote words of truth.

11 The sayings of the wise are like goads, and like nails firmly fixed are the collected sayings which are given by one Shepherd. 12 My son, beware of anything

beyond these. Of making many books there is no end, and much study is a weariness of the flesh.

13 The end of the matter; all has been heard. Fear God, and keep his commandments; for this is the whole duty of man. 14 For God will bring every deed into judgment, with every secret thing, whether good or evil.

Ecclesiastes 12: 1 - 14

These conversations are about faith and knowledge of God. There is a succession of awareness that eventually leads us to the knowledge of the Spirit, which is near to us, and a fellowship, which is possible.

Someone asked me to explain this more thoroughly and I found out I did not do a good job. Let me try with you.

I must quickly explain that I have been raised in a church that has no hard and fast rules such as creeds and complicated doctrines. We have a belief in Jesus Christ and we practice two ordinances or sacraments: baptism and communion. We do not judge anyone beyond the confession of faith that we believe Jesus was the Christ.

But still, what do we mean about soul?

Read the 12th chapter of Ecclesiastes, which is a very definite statement about life, its youth and its conclusion, remembering that its original purpose was to teach a fear of God and to keep the commandments, for this is the whole duty of man.

A long time friend of mine writes a regular newsletter expressing his deep thoughts regarding many theological ideas. In one of his letters he describes being called to conduct a funeral of a neighbor. He writes, "I confess that my theology has been more impacted by my observations of the beach over a lifetime than by my university and seminary training. I've seen the cycles of life and death, the miracle of creation and re-creation, the struggle of the survival of the species, the turning of living creatures into whitened shells. I have pondered the gap between the oyster and myself, and marveled at the fact that my species has the wondrous capacity to be aware, know, wonder, love, and know awe for the very fact of life. On clear nights I look into the stars and think of our Milky Way corner of one of multi-millions of galaxies exploding into existence more than 13 billion years ago. And I think of my brief life span. It is early to think of us as insignificant as the single grain of sand. But something rises in my soul and says, 'Wow! I'm part of something indescribably grand!'" (*Art Morgan Blue Sheet*)

Think about that! Will all the fussing which is again going on about creation – "intelligent design," "life selection," people with little symbols on the bumpers of their cars, fish eating creatures, creatures eating fish – the point is being missed. We are part of something indescribably grand! Our whole duty is to be aware of a relationship we have with that spirit which we call God, and our life is a story of that relationship.

I used to hear my father preach about the wonders of life. He sought to convey them in his preaching and would speak of the fact that when we look into the night sky to see the wonders of the universe and then look into a drop of blood from our finger, we see the same patterns of wonder and life there. And seeing this we worship and give praise for it.

We live in a difficult time, not unusual for there have been many difficult times, ages, conditions, war and peace, confrontation, power plays. But what is power? I have a slip of paper stuck in my computer. It starts with a phrase, "What Is Power?" and it continues – not naked power, nor greed, nor violence, nor mediocrity unexcused, nor treachery, nor deceit. Power is grounded in "God so loved the world."

The author of Ecclesiastes in his time reveals his complete dependence, faith and grounding in God. Listen again to Ecclesiastes 11: 1 – 5:

> 1 Cast your bread upon the waters, for you will find it after many days.
>
> 2 Give a portion to seven, or even to eight, for you know not what evil may happen on earth.
>
> 3 If the clouds are full of rain, they empty themselves on the earth; and if a tree falls to the south or to the north, in the place where the tree falls, there it will lie.
>
> 4 He who observes the wind will not sow; and he who regards the clouds will not reap.

11

5 As you do not know how the spirit comes to the bones in the womb of a woman with child, so you do not know the work of God who makes everything.

The great poem goes on advising the need to clean the mind, release pain from the body, and know the mysteries of life and its vicissitudes. Life is filled with changes, challenges, and through it all wisdom is taught.

While visiting a church in which I had spent some of my youth I asked someone where a particular person was. I was told she had left the church because she was mad at God. There had been some tragedy in her life, loved ones had died too young. This is not an unfamiliar emotion. We shut out so much of the indescribably grand.

It's the old saying, "Cutting off one's nose to spite one's face." How sad. There is so much available and so many can testify to the strength and power they have come to know in the times of crises. Instead they keep God in secret.

I had a friend, a minster older than I, who had served in the army during World War II. He told me of an experience he had. He was in Buchenwald, a place of great atrocities that had been visited upon innocent people, particularly Jews. In viewing the community he came upon the ruins of a synagogue and there sat the rabbi who had managed somehow to survive that hatred and that terror. He sat and visited with the rabbi and was amazed at his faith, his lack of hate, and his trust in God. He knew that he was part of something indescribably grand! And he was not finished with the call he had to proclaim that faith.

The soul is that quiet unseen in us which joins the wonder of an Ecclesiastes and marvels that we are part of something grand. It imbues in us purpose, creation, ability, mind. And we are elevated to a fullness of life awareness, knowledge, love and awe for the very fact of life.

Our Creator,
I have found life is grand.
Thank you for being present and my strength.

A Satisfying Hunger and Thirst

"Blessed are those who hunger and thirst for
righteousness, for they shall be satisfied."

Matthew 5:6

"Henceforth we deem the arrogant blessed; evildoers
not only prosper but when they put God to the test
they escape."

Malachi 3:15

The other day I was in a hurry to go some place or do
something I thought important. It was breakfast and I ate a
piece of toast and drank a cup of coffee and went on my way.
Whatever I was doing it required getting in and out of the
car a number of times, always something which requires extra
energy, walking places, carrying objects, and so on. Before long
I began to have some hunger pangs. Now it must be understood
that I am not a person who goes without nourishment very long
and obviously I have a tendency to over nourish. So, this was
not a usual experience of mine late in the morning. But there
it was and made me wonder what would happen if I ignored it.

I do not have many social pressures or challenges. I move
about rather freely, though income and physical energy do
curtail what I might have done some years ago. Long ago I read
a story about a boy who was running in a cross-country race.
He thought drinking water would slow him down. The truth of
the foolish reasoning made him arrive at his destination in a
serious state of dehydration.

In Matthew 5: 6 Jesus is talking to people who understood
the need for water. It was in short supply and not to be wasted
in a dry and arid land. Here Jesus is talking about something
more than our physical needs. He is talking about a style of

life, a consciousness with which we should live. It is called righteousness.

Righteousness is sometimes an overused description of a good life. It is part of the modern vernacular. Perhaps you've heard of the singing duo, The Righteous Brothers. We are all familiar with a person or persons who being righteous participate in certain rituals or practices, believing these rituals or practices will set them aside from an unrighteous world. In a church I once served there was a couple who proudly proclaimed they tithed. They contributed 10% of their income to the church. But they counted everything, from the amount of gas they used driving to church to the amount of flour in the pie they brought to the potluck supper.

Sometimes the most simplistic reasoning for the troubled world we live in today is that too many people are hungry and thirsty for something and have yet to turn to the serious remedy of their faith.

We thirst for what Jim Wallis, publisher of *Sojourners*, calls "the Common Good." Those of us who seek this are often met with obstacles that block our way and we become frustrated with slow progress. Often goodness seems to receive only passing affirmation. We hear those who offer methods to obtain power and control. During our Civil War, both General Lee and General Grant believed they were doing God's will. I have been preaching for over sixty years and often wonder if I have made any impact. I know I am joined by many like me. But I also know that Jesus unequivocally states that as we hunger and thirst for righteousness we shall be filled. Jesus also says, in Luke 6: 38, "give, and it will be given to you; good measure, pressed down, shaken together, running over, will be put into your lap. For the measure you give will be the measure you get back." The popular song states, "Let there be peace on earth and let it begin with me." Malachi in chapter 4, verse 2, writes that "the sun of righteousness shall rise, with healing in its wings."

Indeed we live in hungry and restless times and we long for solid food and we are restless to find rest with God. As we get older we sometimes live in tighter communities, like retirement communities. We also have neighborhoods of interest. The church and social organizations. Family and professional groups. All are calling on our time and attention. We have short term and long term relationships. Dr. Phil of TV advises that relationships take work, honoring family, neighbors, community, nation. Our highest bliss is giving of ourselves to others. Self-giving love is one of the teachings of Jesus.

I read recently that the U. S. Constitution was written to protect, not to punish. Faith is much the same – to protect and strengthen, not to restrict. It is to show a way, to enhance life. Back in college I had to learn that great poem "The Hound of Heaven" by Francis Thompson:

> Halts by me that footfall:
> Is my gloom, after all,
> Shade of his hand outstretched caressingly?

God is seeking us, to feed our hunger, to quench our thirst.

Our Creator,
I have sat at your table
and fed on the food of life and love.

The Practice of Loyalty

15 When they had finished breakfast, Jesus said to Simon Peter, "Simon, son of John, do you love me more than these?" He said to him, "Yes, Lord; you know that I love you." He said to him, "Feed my lambs." 16 A second time he said to him, "Simon, son of John, do you love me?" He said to him, "Yes, Lord; you know that I love you." He said to him, "Tend my sheep." 17 He said to him the third time, "Simon, son of John, do you love me?" Peter was grieved because he said to him the third time, "Do you love me?" And he said to him, "Lord, you know everything; you know that I love you." Jesus said to him, "Feed my sheep. 18 Truly, truly, I say to you, when you were young, you girded yourself and walked where you would; but when you are old, you will stretch out your hands, and another will gird you and carry you where you do not wish to go." 19 (This he said to show by what death he was to glorify God.) And after this he said to him, "Follow me."

John 21: 15 − 19

David McCullough's book *1776* tells of George Washington seeking to form an army to dispose of the British invasion of the new world. In the beginning he commanded an army of 10,000 men at arms participating in a siege of Boston. But within a year he had less than 2,500 men left. Slowly his soldiers had deserted or died of illness or starvation. And what was true for the Americans was also true for the British troops who had no place to escape, having been brought across the Atlantic in British ships. Loyalty is always a matter of concern for the armies that must confront an enemy, even in the most just conflict. Do we support just the army? Do we support the army and the conflict? Do we support only the conflict? Loyalty is a challenge. We admire those who are loyal. We have questions about those that may or may not consider their activity in some situation, relationship, or challenge as a question of loyalty.

The Bible tells us how Jesus's mother Mary and his brothers request that Jesus return home to his family. He refuses, asking who his family is and implying that all present are indeed his family. And yet at some time we have all experienced separation or alienation from family for a cause or a relationship. In my years of ministry time and again there were those young men or women who broke away from family and traveled a different path. Yet we never know the whole story and we do not always know the complete reason for loyalty or the lack of it.

We who have reached the time of reflection and memories sometimes are in a quandary as to our past decisions. We have much we can reflect upon, much to pass on to others, and at times much for which we need to seek forgiveness. Jesus illustrates to his disciples the immensity of the family of God.

Literary history is filled with this conflict. Shakespeare writes of it in most of his tragedies: *King Lear, Hamlet, Macbeth, Romeo and Juliet.* In American history from the beginning families were torn apart by different loyalties – from the Revolution to the Civil War to both World Wars I and II, to Vietnam. All of this even in the light of what we have been taught and what we have learned from the Scriptures – that we are of one body, joined in history from Abraham, and members of the family of God. We contend over the display or lack of it of the Ten Commandments, yet continue to support leaders in the world who destroy a major commandment, "Thou shall not kill." We worship in a divided faith while we have been told, "There is no distinction between Jew and Greek; the same Lord is Lord of all." We are of a oneness. If there is a reason for loyalty it is a reason of family, a family broader than our immediate knowledge.

A question arises, though. Are intercessory prayers just for special people or do we share them regarding all people, including those who are in conflict?

The author of Hebrews reminds us, "Faith is the assurance of things hoped for, the conviction of things not seen." Stop

19

and think for a moment. There are numbers of churches which exist based on faith, yet faith divided, faith reconstructed, faith of dogma, faith of creed, faith of interpretation, faith of opinion, faith that is open and affirming and faith that is exclusive and restrictive.

Bishop Spong writes, "Our problem is not we are fallen sinners; our problem is that we have not yet become fully human. To speak of a Christ who calls and empowers us to be more deeply and fully human might be the new way to tell that story. One thing is sure, until we find a new way, there is not much hope for a Christian future." That is a difficult statement but we see and experience every day where faith is not so much questioned as it is made into a mandatory belief with no room for speculation or investigation, or wonder. It is once and delivered – not a life long journey of discovery. Paul writes to the Romans: "Let love be genuine: hate what is evil, hold fast to what is good; love one another with brotherly affection: outdo one another in showing honor. Never flag in zeal, be aglow with the Spirit, serve the Lord. Rejoice in your hope, be patient in tribulation, be constant in prayer. Contribute to the needs of the saints, practice hospitality."

That's a challenge central to loyalty – not names, phrases, ritual, creeds, dogma, but belief and practice of the simple Word. The Disciples of Christ, what we call the New Testament Church, had many challenges and many problems as it began to grow in its knowledge and in a world much larger than the little bit of community in the East. With growth came expansion, with growth came new ideas, with growth came temptations and confrontation. It continues today. Voices all around us constantly call us in other directions, hold out to us formulas for new ways of living, hold out to us that we must be vigilant, suspicious, careful, and maybe these voices of warning are the very insidious divisive intruders into our loyalty.

I once knew a young man writing for a small local paper often in what he called "defense of the Gospel." He felt that some recent scholarship and growth in awareness and understanding were not so much growth as a detriment to faith. In a conversation with him I contended that the Gospel needed no defense. It needed constant study and learning. Franklin

Delano Roosevelt's statement during the Great Depression that we have nothing to fear but fear itself is relevant today. To look upon the world with the eyes of fear and to be constantly on the defense against new learning will bring the very destruction that we fear. Greater knowledge in this day will happen when we become loyal to the fact that we are never finished learning. There is yet more truth to break forth.

Let's open our lives to the simple pronouncements of Jesus and his belief in love and loyalty to the family of God. To divert from that loyalty, to abandon it for a conquering world adrift in the flesh that Paul describes in Galatians – a world of immorality, impurity, licentiousness, idolatry, sorcery, enmity, strife, jealousy, anger, selfishness, dissension, party spirit, and envy – will bring that which the prophets of doom and gloom preach.

The formula of loyalty is clear and codified. It is our decision to follow it.

Our Creator,
as you have spoken in the Good Samaritan,
speak in me so my loyalty may serve you.

All in a Family: *Father's Day*

Today is Father's Day, the flip side of the Sunday observance in May of Mother's Day. One of the popular ultra right talk radio personalities was complaining the other day because there were, he said, "liberal" churches using the term "Parents' Day" for each of these holidays. Most of these radio personalities don't know what they are talking about. It is obvious that even with large research staffs, they don't do their homework. The history of both these observances, Mother's Day and Father's Day, does not go back too far in time. One was thought up by a woman who wanted to honor her mother, a loyal and ardent teacher of children. The other, however, was an obvious creation of the retail industry, which didn't want to lose a good sales opportunity.

Very frankly there used to be, and sometimes still is, a problem using the word "Father" as a name for God. For what do you do when teaching children whose father is absent, abusive, or inattentive? What is more, the term can sometimes be seen as sexist.

Yet the scriptures often use the term to describe God. The early translators of the scriptures, the codifiers, felt this was the best description. Using a *Cruden's Concordance* as a quick guide we do find that almost half a page records places in the scriptures where the word "Father" is used. That is in both the Old and the New Testament. I am sure that most of us are familiar with John 10:30: "I and the Father are one." And also Matthew 11: 27: "All things have been delivered to me by my Father; and no one knows the Son except the Father . . ." We are also familiar with the idea that Abraham is the father of nations and the patriarch of three great faiths: Christianity, Judaism, and Islam. This is an idea that seems to have been lost on all sides but is reemerging in some churches.

23

Cruden's Concordance goes on to list those places where reference is made to "Her Father," "His Father," "Our Father, and "Their Father." Today in some churches the famous "Gloria Patria or "Glory to the Father" is being sung as "Glory be to the Creator" in a desire to keep sexual preferences from our great affirmations of faith that God is creator or as Paul Tillich has said, "Ground of all being."

Interestingly enough I grew up in a church where much was made of Mother's Day and not much of Father's Day. In fact when I began to preach, next to Easter and Christmas Sundays, Mother's Day was the largest in attendance. I don't know if it is still the custom, as it was early in my ministry, to wear a white rose to honor a mother who was deceased and a red rose for a living mother. At least today we have an ugly tie contest on Father's Day.

These observances were not all bad, though they seem to have changed over the years. They were not always good either. I can remember as a child that my father, also a preacher, was expected to preach a tear-jerker sermon on Mother's Day. He believed that he felt his mother's presence in the pulpit with him Sunday. I have never had such an experience, even though many times in preparing a sermon memories of both my father's and mother's teaching come to me.

Let us go on beyond the family stories that we all have regarding our parents and look at a much larger picture. We are all familiar with Mark 3: 31 − 35: "And his mother and his brothers came; and standing outside they sent to him and called him. And a crowd was sitting about him; and they said to him, 'Your mother and your brothers are outside, asking for you.' And he replied, 'Who are my mother and my brothers?' And looking around on those who sat about him, he said, 'Here are my mother and my brothers! Whoever does the will of God is my brother, and sister, and mother.'"

Again, when I was a boy and early in my ministry our church, The Christian Church (Disciples of Christ), used an all-inclusive term of The Brotherhood. We have stopped doing so, in order to take sexism out of our language, and yet perhaps we have lost something by that. For this did teach something: that we are indeed family. We are one. If you wish to work this a bit harder consider Paul's admonishing in 1 Corinthians 12: 12 -13: "For just as the body is one and has many members, and all the members of the body, though many, are one body, so it is with Christ. For by one Spirit we were all baptized into one body – Jews or Greeks, slaves or free – and all were made to drink of one Spirit." That is why we have always opened our communion, not examining those in attendance, not excluding any who wish to partake or participate in the worship. There is a connection between us all.

The authors of the Old Testament knew all this. They write a story about the beginning and though there are two stories about the creation in Genesis, we see a common thread of a connection, a common ground, a mutual creation, Paul Tillich's "Ground of all being." There is a common beginning, a mutual inheritance.

Today the sciences, like archeology, are constantly digging up evidence of the long inheritance we have with one another. How the movement of humans developed the land upon which we live. How nature, food, geography, harvest, masses of animals caused our forebears to move about the earth. But in spite of differences we see today that some place there was a beginning, some place common ancestors that gave us common features, blood types, genetic patterns. We are one, and Jesus is saying to his disciples and all disciples that to join with him gives an even greater identity to our personhood, our conditions, and our future.

Remember the situation comedy "All in the Family"? It was screened in an era when there were efforts being made to bring about a culture and society of many groups into an understanding of one another. It is sad that these efforts were heavily abused by critics. Many were afraid that they would lose something if such a philosophy were true, or that their citizenship and nationality would be destroyed rather than enhanced. I was part of an era when the church sought to have greater cooperation with others. We wanted to bring about a union, a uniting of Christians into a common goal. What happened? Where is that movement today? What we see instead are mega-churches, bigger and better, places that are virtually religious entertainment, opinionated in their approach to society, judgmental and condemning. Independent from any sort of cooperation, unity, common belief they say, "We are the only ones, we are the true church, only here will you find salvation." How much are they really part of the whole family of God?

When you belong to a family you know that within the family there may be differences of opinion, manners, interest. For example, I have in my immediate family two children involved in the fine arts, one an artist, the other a writer, and a third who likes to run marathons. I have no clue where any of that comes from! But still we are family. And thus when Jesus is asked what he wants to do about his family, standing out on the edge, saying he must come home, he asks, "Who are my mother and my brothers?" Those who are doing the will of God are mother, brother, sister, family.

We refer to a place like this as a community, with a variety of conditions, a variety of interests and beliefs. All the same, here you are one, you are part of a whole and you learn to live in close proximity, eat in a common room, share the hall space, the lounge, and the grounds as one. It may be difficult at times but to adjust and to appreciate makes it move livable.

In our history, then, we have had many fathers, many mothers, many parents. And going back, far far back, we will find a common ground.

Our Creator,
blessed be your family.
Open to me the depth and width
of this great family that I may praise them.

Salt of the Earth

They called Jesus "Rabbi" or "Teacher," and he made faith live, teaching a way of life, making disciples and also teachers. In a moment while teaching he said the disciples were the "salt of the earth." That was an ultimate compliment. They understood this compliment meant "worth," "value," something good, important, and necessary to life. As we get older we sometimes fall into a mental state of believing we no longer have worth, that our saltness has lost its vigor, lost the ability to add something good to others and ourselves.

Here's a new version of the famous Serenity Prayer: "God grant me the serenity to accept the people I cannot change, the courage to change the people I can, and the wisdom to know it's me."

Have you ever read the lengthy list of individuals in the scriptures having serious faults? The list is long and contains such names as Noah, who was drunk, Jeremiah and Timothy, who were too young, Job, who was bankrupt, and Zaccheus, who was too short.

Jesus knew the potential of his disciples and challenged them in spite of their faults to follow a special way of life.

I understand growing older and the many things I am no longer able to do and the compensations I must make. During a recent trip to Europe I had to use a wheelchair many times. It was, in fact, an asset, and I found myself admitted to the head of the line many times. Have you ever stood at the famous Mona Lisa almost close enough to touch it?

Of course, there are times my memory fails and I tell something more than once. Of course, I have a granddaughter who is quick to say, "Yes, Grandpa, you told me that!" And yet we must all be quick to remember that we are part of a creation that is valuable and loved.

Writing to the Colossians, Paul states, "Conduct yourselves wisely toward outsiders, making the most of the time. Let your speech always be gracious, seasoned with salt, so that you know how you ought to answer every one." (Colossians 4: 6)

I have moved a number of times and even lived in a country other than my own. In each place I had to learn how to live with neighbors. In some places it was easy, in others it took a bit of adjustment. More than once I needed to be the salt of the earth, accept change, adjust to a new community, culture, habits, and life style.

Emmet Fox, a spiritual leader of the early 20th century, once said, "If you understand and accept the teachings of Jesus; and make every effort to practice them in every department of your daily life; if you seek systematically to destroy in yourself everything which should not be there – not feeding or nursing it by giving into it, but starving it by refusing it expression; if you extend the right thought loyally to every person or thing within your ken, especially to the people or things you dislike; then you are worthy to be called salt of the earth."

Life is one of relationships. Jesus talked to his disciples about important relationships with God. Not with authorities in religion or state, but relationships with God, the ground of life joining with creation. In a humorous way consider this:

- God wants spiritual fruit, not nuts.
- Dear God, I have a problem. It's me.
- Growing old is inevitable. Growing up is optional.
- Faith is the ability to not panic.
- As a child of God, prayer is like calling home every day.

Each of us has potential; its intensity, size, and challenge changes with time and ability. We are never without a challenge, never without a place to make a difference, and we seek constantly the idea of fulfillment.

In spite of age there is potential. The major theme of these meditations is that we are never ending. We must be like Job who, though he appeared to lose all, came to the conclusion that "I have heard you by the ear, now I see you with my eye."

Serious looking in faith will open your eyes to the salt of the earth.

29

Our Creator,
It is blessed to be Salt of the Earth.
Continue to strengthen me that I may give
strength, honor, and love to your family.

First Day of Life

1 When Jesus had spoken these words, he lifted up his eyes to heaven and said, "Father, the hour has come; glorify thy Son that the Son may glorify thee, 2 since thou hast given him power over all flesh, to give eternal life to all whom thou hast given him. 3 And this is eternal life, that they know thee the only true God, and Jesus Christ whom thou hast sent. 4 I glorified thee on earth, having accomplished the work which thou gavest me to do; 5 and now, Father, glorify thou me in thy own presence with the glory which I had with thee before the world was made.

6 "I have manifested thy name to the men whom thou gavest me out of the world; thine they were, and thou gavest them to me, and they have kept thy word. 7 Now they know that everything that thou hast given me is from thee; 8 for I have given them the words which thou gavest me, and they have received them and know in truth that I came from thee; and they have believed that thou didst send me. 9 I am praying for them; I am not praying for the world but for those whom thou hast given me, for they are thine; 10 all mine are thine, and thine are mine, and I am glorified in them. 11 And now I am no more in the world, but they are in the world, and I am coming to thee. Holy Father, keep them in thy name, which thou hast given me, that they may be one, even as we are one. 12 While I was with them, I kept them in thy name, which thou hast given me; I have guarded them, and none of them is lost but the son of perdition, that the scripture might be fulfilled. 13 But now I am coming to thee; and these things I

speak in the world, that they may have my joy fulfilled in themselves. 14 I have given them thy word; and the world has hated them because they are not of the world, even as I am not of the world. 15 I do not pray that thou shouldst take them out of the world, but that thou shouldst keep them from the evil one. 16 They are not of the world, even as I am not of the world. 17 Sanctify them in the truth; thy word is truth. 18 As thou didst send me into the world, so I have sent them into the world. 19 And for their sake I consecrate myself, that they also may be consecrated in truth.

John 17: 1 – 19

When the calendar changes at the end of December, we make a stab at resolutions regarding the coming year. I stand and look at my garden and speculate what it will be in the spring. I look at a list of books I can print on my computer and decide what I wish to read. When I was preaching regularly I made a draft of subjects and scriptures to cover in the coming year. In spite of all the planning and what-if's, changes come along anyway.

The so called spam on my computer is constantly reminding me that there are people and organizations seeking me to make changes. As I sat writing this meditation it was trash pick up day. I remember as a child men walking along the street picking up heavy containers and dumping them into an open truck. Now I can see a big green truck and everything is mechanical. Change happens. The driver never leaves the truck.

Have you driven a new car lately? Can you remember the first you drove? What changes have happened?

I am a reader of Civil War history. John McPherson in *Battle Cry of Freedom* states, "The hallmark of the U. S. has been growth. Americans have typically defined this process in quantitative terms. Never was that so true than in the first half of the 19th century, when the unparalleled rate of growth took place in three dimensions: population, territory, and economy." At the same time there were many left behind. The growth had good and bad results for selected ethnic groups and age groups. Wars continued and differences in territorial conquest took the lives of civilians and military. Of course, certain advances in research and production benefited. Also around the same time as the Civil War there were changes in religion.

Today we continue to seek some certainty about life and we are bombarded with new ideas in politics, industry, medicine, society, and relationships. Religion and belief are also involved. A few years ago a group of evangelists began to promote the Bible as written in code. They sold lots of books and it is strange how all that has become very quiet. Such speculation is not new. In the 1950's there were those who believed certain words in the Bible were symbols for the Soviet Union. But strangely enough those translations have faded with time and scholarship.

The question at the beginning of each new season remains, "What is before us?" In short there is still much to do and much to change. And while it is adventurous to learn of the exploration of Mars, it is far more important to explore and solve the mystery of Alzheimer's, poverty, nutrition, and yes, aging.

Jesus talking to his disciples in what has become his farewell says nothing about preparing for war, power struggles, or obtaining the upper hand globally. His lesson is not in code. It is simple, straightforward, positive, productive, and based on plain common sense.

So, what do we say? We say, "What can I do?" It's a difficult question. Sometimes we who are of advanced age feel the best thing is to go off and sit in a rocking chair and do nothing. But there is a way, sadly not always practiced in American culture. It is called "saging." In many cultures the elderly are held in a place of honor. Experience through trial and error gives them special knowledge for those who seek to make changes. And there must be the practice of looking for change, trying something new.

Story-telling is a time honored way of looking at life in both directions. Here is a story my son has told me:

A duck walks into a bar and asks, "Got any grapes?" The bartender says, "No, this is a bar. I don't have any grapes." The duck does this every day for three days and every time the bartender tells him there are no grapes in his bar. Finally, he warns the duck that if he asks once more, he will nail the duck's bill to the bar. The next day the duck walks in and asks, "Got any nails?" "No!" the bartender says. "I don't have any nails." The duck asks, "Got any grapes?"

Persistence does pay and sometimes it is necessary to be persistent.

Jesus says to his father God about his followers: "The glory which thou has given me I have given to them, that they may be one even as we are one, I in them and thou in me, that they may become perfectly one, so that the world may know that thou has sent me and hast loved them even as thou has loved me." (John 17: 22 – 23)

In a changing world we continue to look for grapes believing they will heal when what we need to look for is right before us. We can live with change. We can bring the left behind with us. We can continue to be sages reminding the world we are all in God, born in his creation.

Our Creator,
you were present at my birth, present in my youth,
present in my years of responsibility.
Now I am strengthened and blessed
to believe in your continued love.

Communion with God and His Creation

And God said, "Behold, I have given you every plant yielding seed which is upon the face of all the earth, and every tree with seed in its fruit; you shall have them for food."

Genesis 1: 29

And God saw everything that he had made, and behold, it was very good. And there was evening and there was morning, a sixth day.

Genesis 1: 31

Jesus said to them, "I am the bread of life; he who comes to me shall not hunger, and he who believes in me shall never thirst."

John 6: 35

When I was a boy I lived in the parsonage. In most Midwestern towns the parsonage was always next door to the church. It was a traditional Ohio house – two stories with an attic and a porch extending across the front of the house. When you entered the front door you stood in an entry way; to the left was the living room and behind that the dining room. Up stairs three bed rooms and the bath.

That dining room was significant because, as retired Professor Keith Watkins has written, we are "a table-centered church." This does not mean we eat a lot. It means that Communion at the Lord's Table is an act of worship each Sunday.

These meditations were originally written because once a month I presented both devotions and Communion at a retirement village in Oregon. In weekly worship we believed Communion was the central act of worship.

The observing of the Communion can be very elaborate or very simple. In my Scottish pastorate the table was central and the passing of the cup from hand to hand was done in complete silence. I also had the opportunity to attend a Passover seder in a Jewish home and much of what is done during our Communion is rooted in that history.

Communion contributes a great sense of awe, spiritual closeness, community, and observation of a spiritual presence. In a book called *Whose Freedom? The Battle over America's Important Idea*, there is an explanation of direct causation and systematic response. One is how we respond to direct demand. Someone says "Jump!" And we respond, "How high?" The other is the complex result of many experiences we have day to day.

At the table, as a community event or even a family experience, we share in a simple meal. We pass hand to hand. We serve one another and become the priesthood of faith. What we have learned, observed, and practiced is melded together and in that togetherness we have a sense of presence, a sense of history, a sense of a life that is taught and shared.

It is not far to seek how this worship experience has over the centuries taken on ritual, mystery, and in some places simplicity. In all places it is telling and sharing the same revelation, fellowship, and redemption.

In our devotional times, meditations, sharing and breaking bread, sharing the cup, we can contemplate that we are involved in something special, strong, spiritual. These communal events represent not only time and presence. They represent that we are an extension of the ministry of Christ. That ministry is grounded deeply in the revelation of love to be shared by all.

Creation all around me, I feel your presence.
I am a part of something grand.
I praise you for the times
I have been able to commune with you.

On Reflection

1 Remember also your Creator in the days of your youth, before the evil days come, and the years draw night, when you will say, "I have no pleasure in them";

2 before the sun and the light and the moon and the stars are darkened and the clouds return after the rain; 3 in the day when the keepers of the house tremble, and the strong men are bent, and the grinders cease because they are few, and those that look through the windows are dimmed, 4 and the doors on the street are shut; when the sound of the grinding is low, and one rises up at the voice of a bird, and all the daughters of song are brought low; 5 they are afraid also of what is high, and terrors are in the way; the almond tree blossoms, the grasshopper drags itself along and desire fails; because man goes to his eternal home, and the mourners go about the streets; 6 before the silver cord is snapped, or the golden bowl is broken, or the pitcher is broken at the fountain, or the wheel broken at the cistern, 7 and the dust returns to the earth as it was, and the spirit returns to God who gave it. 8 Vanity of vanities, says the Preacher; all is vanity.

Ecclesiastes 12: 1 – 8

We cannot help but contemplate our aging. All it takes is to pick up a book of photos and see ourselves. Most of the time inside my head I am no different than I was, say, fifty years ago. And then the mirror gets in the way or I find myself pushing and huffing to get out of a chair that is too low to the floor, or I attend my aerobic and strength class at the senior center, and I am quickly reminded that there are many things I can no longer do, even if I have passed some of the tests at the center with high marks.

My father in his last years often said, "Getting old is hell."

I have spent a considerable time studying gerontology, and I have lectured on the subject, written on it, held seminars on it, and yet when that is the subject of a presentation I look at the guest speaker and he or she is younger than I. How comes it that all this knowledge I have, this book learning, this experience is now thought to be of no use and I am not the guest speaker, the authority?

In preparation for this book, I turned to an old tried and true scripture to remind me of what I am not experiencing. The Preacher, Ecclesiastes, said it best:

"Remember also your Creator in the days of your youth, before the evil days come, and the years draw night, when you will say, 'I have no pleasure in them.'" Not very pleasant advice. And now that I am among that group I decided to say something about it.

Older adults have always interested me. In my experience they many times were the backbone of the congregation. Many of them had become sages instead of just old folks. I wish to share with you some ideas and inspiration regarding our lives, which we all need when we enter into that special society of senior citizens. For example, recently speaking to you, some guest who had come along to help me asked if I was going to be inspirational. I said, "I hope so." But when the time was over and later when we were at dinner, I asked the one who questioned me if she had been inspired, she bluntly told me, "No." One other guest was critical, too, saying that I seemed to be unfinished.

Only later did I reflect upon what I should have said in the first place. Years ago when I was a very young minister only recently out of seminary and pastoring my first church I had the occasion to be invited to fill in at a major church while I was on vacation. I was very nervous about it because I knew that my philosophy professor would be present. I told my father, a very eloquent and inspirational preacher, and he said to me, "Relax, be yourself. If you try to preach to your philosophy professor, you will not preach to the rest of the congregation." This was not to say they were not as intelligent as the professor, but it was to say that the simple straightforward preaching was good for everyone. And so I should have said to my critics on that previous occasion, "If I had just preached to you, I might not have preached to the others present."

It's not that an older adult sermon needs to be preached every Sunday, but an understanding of the wholeness of the Gospel does.

Let us in our brief time together just take the time to consider some of the subjects which concern us in our older adult years. I will start with this: I have two important documents which I am required to carry on my person. One: my Social Security number. Two: my Medicare card. Furthermore, I need to register with a pharmacy. I have been involved in gerontology for many years, but I am confused regarding some of these things. Often I receive my medications without payment, but recently a medication called for a co-payment of just under $100.

Hear these words from the Preacher in Ecclesiastes: "before the sun and the light and the moon and the stars are darkened and the clouds return after the rain; in the day when the keepers of the house tremble . . ." In other words, your health will be challenged whether you like it or not.

And so I keep my appointments at the doctor's. I check my blood pressure. I take my pills no matter what they cost. I go to aerobics classes twice a week. And the rest of the week I try to recover from the aches and pains. Health is an important issue.

Last week Sharon and I rearranged a room where we both have computers and where I sometimes paint. Lots of information comes from the computer and I do most of my banking and bill paying, saving me hours and gas. Living on a fixed income takes energy and caution. It is good to take some classes to be advised by a competent and honest financial planner. I did this for a few years, lecturing around the Northwest on planning for retirement. But even after one retires, these are particular days with rising prices and politicians believing those retired or not working are lazy and without motivation. And the Scriptures call out for "aid to the least of these." When was the last time you heard a preacher speak to that subject, particularly on radio or television?

I don't mean to be negative, only to say that we should be aware and cautious and not believe everything we hear. I regret to say that we who are older need to continue to read, continue to be alert and have trust in those who are important.

While I was writing this devotional, Sharon was sitting at her computer. We live on a cul-de-sac and children play in it. Our neighbors are my daughter, her husband, and three children. Sharon and I share eleven grandchildren, and it's a joy to have three of them living next door. We used to hear the door close when they were all in school. Now they are off to university and the street is quiet. But it was beginning to be quiet anyway as I came to discover that I needed hearing aids and now wear them faithfully.

There are two lessons and concerns here. Enjoy your family and if you are fortunate, enjoy the grandchildren and the great grandchildren. But one thing I have learned is that if they wish information from me or advice, they will ask for it. I try not to be constantly teaching, though it is hard for me not to be.

Finally, I speak on Faith. The Preacher in Ecclesiastes does this: "Besides being wise, the Preacher also taught the people knowledge, weighing and studying and arranging proverbs with great care." Continue to learn, continue to be interested, even though you may never be asked for advice because you are considered old. In your own heart you know you know. God is an awesome God. God always has much to reveal and much to show you and much to give you. Most of all it is love which you can share with others, people in your community, family, friends. Look upon the world that God has made and placed you in and enjoy its goods. What does it say in Genesis after each moment of creation? "And it was good." And so it is.

Age does not interfere with the knowledge that God is a God of love. And it is good.

Our Creator,
I reflect on my life and its journeys.
In all times and all events of life
I know you have been with me.

Release the Captive

1 They came to the other side of the sea, to the country of the Ger'asenes. 2 And when he had come out of the boat, there met him out of the tombs a man with an unclean spirit, 3 who lived among the tombs; and no one could bind him any more, even with a chain; 4 for he had often been bound with fetters and chains, but the chains he wrenched apart, and the fetters he broke in pieces; and no one had the strength to subdue him. 5 Night and day among the tombs and on the mountains he was always crying out, and bruising himself with stones. 6 And when he saw Jesus from afar, he ran and worshiped him; 7 and crying out with a loud voice, he said, "What have you to do with me, Jesus, Son of the Most High God? I adjure you by God, do not torment me." 8 For he had said to him, "Come out of the man, you unclean spirit!" 9 And Jesus asked him, "What is your name?" He replied, "My name is Legion; for we are many." 10 And he begged him eagerly not to send them out of the country. 11 Now a great herd of swine was feeding there on the hillside; 12 and they begged him, "Send us to the swine, let us enter them." 13 So he gave them leave. And the unclean spirits came out, and entered the swine; and the herd, numbering about two thousand, rushed down the steep bank into the sea, and were drowned in the sea.

14 The herdsmen fled, and told it in the city and in the country. And people came to see what it was that had happened. 15 And they came to Jesus, and saw the demoniac sitting there, clothed and in his right mind, the man who had had the legion; and they were afraid.

16 And those who had seen it told what had happened to the demoniac and to the swine. 17 And they began to beg Jesus to depart from their neighborhood. 18 And as he was getting into the boat, the man who had been possessed with demons begged him that he might be with him. 19 But he refused, and said to him, "Go home to your friends, and tell them how much the Lord has done for you, and how he has had mercy on you." 20 And he went away and began to proclaim in the Decap'olis how much Jesus had done for him; and all men marveled.

Mark 5: 1 – 20

"The Spirit of the Lord is upon me,
because he has anointed me to preach
    good news to the poor.
He has sent me to proclaim release to the captives
and recovering of sight to the blind,
to set at liberty those who are oppressed . . ."

Luke 4: 18

The Spirit of the Lord GOD is upon me,
because the LORD has anointed me
    to bring good tidings to the afflicted;
        he has sent me to bind up the broken-hearted,
    to proclaim liberty to the captives,
        and the opening of the prison to those who are
          bound;
    to proclaim the year of the LORD's favor,
        and the day of vengeance of our God;
    to comfort all who mourn . . .

Isaiah 61: 1 – 2

I wish to call your attention to two scriptures today. One is a favorite of mine and I often refer to it in my devotions. In fact, I look upon it as Jesus' ordination sermon. Having been in the wilderness and been baptized by John, he now attends the synagogue where he opens the book of Isaiah and reads the famous text regarding the spirit of the Lord and what he intends to do.

The next scripture is one about healing a demonic man imprisoned in a cave and calling out for help, recognizing that Jesus is a special person and appealing to him for help. Which Jesus gives him. Indeed, Jesus releases him from the captivity of his illness and the imprisonment of his body.

I believe very strongly that this first scripture is the center of Jesus' ministry and that it is the motto and outline of what is expected of any of us who claim to be his followers. When we in worship express our belief in Jesus Christ we are taking upon ourselves the outline of this sermon and the commands it makes upon us.

The first scripture is the command, the instruction, of what our lives must be. The second scripture is telling us that in the most dire circumstances we can be released from that which captures us, impedes us, and stands in our way of living a full and accomplished life.

So often in our lives we feel as if we are captive. This is particularly true as we age and body, mind, vision, all seem to place us in a cave, bound and hampered.

I am determined to understand the instruction of Jesus that indeed it is possible to overcome that captivity and live ways in which my life is still rich, productive, and meaningful.

I am a fan of Judi Dench – Dame Judi Dench having been honored by the Queen of England. I was insulted when I read recently, or heard it said, that Judi had been disinvited from two morning talk shows because she was too old and would not appeal to the younger set being courted by Good Morning America and The View.

A good part of the captivity that we feel has been thrust upon us by the media, fashion, and marketing.

I like to paint. It is, in fact, an avocation which I have taken up later in my life and pretty much since I retired. For a long time I attended classes and belonged to associations of adult artists that gave me ideas and shared methods. It was often a mix of younger and older artists enjoying the fine art of painting.

There are so many people today put in boxes, made to stay in places that are contrary to their own mindset. And they have often allowed this to happen. It is time for us all to accept and believe that we are liberated, free, and out of the box to continue to learn, experience, understand the world in which we live and make our contribution. The chains are released and we are constantly called to new and expanded awareness.

There are times I regret that I am no longer preaching on a regular basis. After doing it over 50 years I often longed to have the relief of not turning out a sermon every week. When I first began to preach I was just out of college and in seminary. I was called to a little country church in Kentucky. Consider the fact that as a new preacher, even though I had grown up in the parsonage, I had some pretty hard acts to follow. And when I invited my very experienced father, a man who had great passages of scripture memorized, to come and hold a revival meeting for me, I had a doubly hard act to follow. Now in my senior years the chains are loose and I believe that you and I have some important things to say and share. In spite of prejudice and in spite of the rapid pace of the world about us and the changes that are taking place, we still have much to say, much to do, and much to share.

Oh, I know sometimes we bore our children and grandchildren. My granddaughter is quick to tell me if I have told her some story over again. So be it. But she knows I am there for her, and I and her grandmother are sources of reference, supply and support.

Take a little notepad and jot down a list of prayer concerns each day. Pause and read it often. Know in your heart you are contributing to the care of someone or something you love.

Times are a-changing and we can contribute to a change which is good, nurturing, loving, and supportive. Every age is different and every age can have both the negative and the positive. Today, sadly enough, there are those who are spewing out hate, division, falsehood, lies, and seek to destroy any advances which have been made in humankind. In some places the comfortable champion hatred and seek to place others, who are different, in tight boxes, not allowing them to come out. A good portion of my ministerial history was spent in the dark days of racial disharmony. Headway has been made because there are those who believe that the captive should be released, that the acceptable day of the Lord has indeed come and we must dwell in it and support the healing.

But most of all we must do it for ourselves. We who are in what is called the senior years must not only accept who we are, we must not allow anyone, and that includes ourselves, to place us in a box, to chain us, to imprison us because of some shallow false prejudice which stereotypes us and makes us believe that it, rather than we, knows what is best for us and thus confines us, ghettoizes us, claims we have served our usefulness and thus should merely sit in a rocking chair and watch the sunset. It was once said of a distant relative of mine that in his retirement he sat on the porch and owned the whole world but never got up to claim it. We still have much to claim, much not only to own but develop, beautify, share and give.

Read the Bible. See the stories of those in advanced age doing marvelous things. Let it be said of us at the inevitable end we have fought the good fight, run the race, and kept the faith. In other words, we must keep swinging!

In the fifth chapter of Mark, what did Jesus do to the man he healed? That man wanted to join the group, and Jesus instead gave him another assignment. If the world is changing, and it is, then we with the information, the maturity, the insight and the wisdom are not charged to keep things as they are. We are charged to call for sensibility, insight, for planning, for faith, for the whole commandment which Jesus said is the newest – to love God with all our hearts and our neighbors as ourselves.

For a very brief time I knew and communicated with the famous doctor Elisabeth Kübler Ross. I visited in her home and she in mine. I exchanged Christmas cards and though I lost contact with her in later years, I would read now and then that this most compassionate person continued, even in debilitating infirmity, to bring hope, vision, care to those in the final years of their lives. One time when she was in a community lecturing, a friend of mine went up to her and told her of a tragic incident to one of his grandchildren. She told him to stay with her for a few moments and then took my friend aside and talked with him, counseled with him, comforted and nurtured him. After those few moments, he went away healed from the great hurt that he had carried for so many years over the tragedy.

We never know when we shall be called upon to give some word, some touch, some wisdom. And we will give it, share it, release the captive when we are willing to release ourselves and know that wisdom is always at hand and we will have much to give even in every age. The Spirit is upon us to give the Good News.

Our Creator,
truly the Spirit of the Lord has been with me.
It has enabled me to continue
the ministry Jesus Christ began.

Breakfast with Jesus

After this Jesus revealed himself again to the disciples by the Sea of Tibe´ri-as; and he revealed himself in this way. 2 Simon Peter, Thomas called the Twin, Nathan´a-el of Cana in Galilee, the sons of Zeb´edee, and two others of his disciples were together. 3 Simon Peter said to them, "I am going fishing." They said to him, "We will go with you." They went out and got into the boat; but that night they caught nothing.

4 Just as day was breaking, Jesus stood on the beach; yet the disciples did not know that it was Jesus. 5 Jesus said to them, "Children, have you any fish?" They answered him, "No." 6 He said to them, "Cast the net on the right side of the boat, and you will find some." So they cast it, and now they were not able to haul it in, for the quantity of fish. 7 That disciple whom Jesus loved said to Peter, "It is the Lord!" When Simon Peter heard that it was the Lord, he put on his clothes, for he was stripped for work, and sprang into the sea. 8 But the other disciples came in the boat, dragging the net full of fish, for they were not far from the land, but about a hundred yards off.

9 When they got out on land, they saw a charcoal fire there, with fish lying on it, and bread. 10 Jesus said to them, "Bring some of the fish that you have just caught." 11 So Simon Peter went aboard and hauled the net ashore, full of large fish, a hundred and fifty-three of them; and although there were so many, the net was not torn. 12 Jesus said to them, "Come and have breakfast." Now none of the disciples dared ask him, "Who are you?" They knew it was the Lord. 13 Jesus came and

took the bread and gave it to them, and so with the fish. 14 This was now the third time that Jesus was revealed to the disciples after he was raised from the dead.

Jesus and Peter

15 When they had finished breakfast, Jesus said to Simon Peter, "Simon, son of John, do you love me more than these?" He said to him, "Yes, Lord; you know that I love you." He said to him, "Feed my lambs." 16 A second time he said to him, "Simon, son of John, do you love me?" He said to him, "Yes, Lord; you know that I love you." He said to him, "Tend my sheep." 17 He said to him the third time, "Simon, son of John, do you love me?" Peter was grieved because he said to him the third time, "Do you love me?" And he said to him, "Lord, you know everything; you know that I love you." Jesus said to him, "Feed my sheep. 18 Truly, truly, I say to you, when you were young, you girded yourself and walked where you would; but when you are old, you will stretch out your hands, and another will gird you and carry you where you do not wish to go." 19 (This he said to show by what death he was to glorify God.) And after this he said to him, "Follow me."

John 21: 1 – 19

9 But Saul, still breathing threats and murder against the disciples of the Lord, went to the high priest 2 and asked him for letters to the synagogues at Damascus, so that if he found any belonging to the Way, men or women, he might bring them bound to Jerusalem. 3 Now as he journeyed he approached Damascus, and suddenly a light from heaven flashed about him. 4 And he fell to the ground and heard a voice saying to him, "Saul, Saul, why do you persecute me?" 5 And he said, "Who are you, Lord?" And he said, "I am Jesus, whom you are persecuting; 6 but rise and enter the city, and you will be told what you are to do." 7 The men who were traveling with him stood speechless, hearing the voice but seeing no one. 8 Saul arose from the ground;

and when his eyes were opened, he could see nothing; so they led him by the hand and brought him into Damascus. 9 And for three days he was without sight, and neither ate nor drank.

10 Now there was a disciple at Damascus named Anani'as. The Lord said to him in a vision, "Anani'as." And he said, "Here I am, Lord."

Acts 9: 1 – 10

The Disciples are confused with previous events, the crucifixion, the risen Christ and now his visit at Tiberius. Fred Craddock, the late distinguished professor of preaching and Disciples of Christ minister, has stated about the celebration of Easter: "By crowding the celebration into one day rather than 50, the season was robbed of the time necessary to ponder the meaning of resurrection, to wait in prayer, to experience Christ's continuing presence. In other words, Easter was aborted rather than continued to its completion on Pentecost Sunday. Pentecost fulfills Easter, and without Pentecost the church cannot shout, 'He is risen!' loudly enough to sustain the people of God week after week."

The scripture from John is part of a group of Easter experiences telling the victory and the future of faith. We can speculate on three important lessons.

- Peter seeks to evade what he experiences by going off fishing. He seeks to escape, only to be called back.
- We see the resurrected Christ waiting on the shore and Jesus prepares breakfast. Is this a "table" event?
- The risen Christ challenges his Disciples, through Peter, to care for His sheep.

Faith is illustrated in this story as both contemplative and active.

Consider the idea of presence. In Catholicism, they teach about transubstantiation. That is also a concept of a living presence of the Christ. In the regular act of the Lord's Supper, we are living in action again and again and telling the message of Christ. We are again asked the question he asked Peter: "Do you love me?" And again told, "Care for my sheep." The important part of this message is that something is required beyond the contemplative, something must happen; we must be agents of change, of caring love.

Before I became a minster and clear back to my high school days I learned from Micah: "He has showed you, O man, what is good; and what does the Lord required of you but to do justice, and to love kindness, and to walk humbly with your God?"

There is a call for action throughout the scriptures. Ministering is not a specialty requiring advanced education. It is a calling of faith. When we practice communion, we pass the bread and cup to one another, a symbol of the priesthood of all believers.

Remember these verses from Psalm 30:

Sing praises to the LORD O you saints,
    and give thanks to his holy name.
For his anger is but for a moment,
    and his favor is for a lifetime.
Weeping may tarry for the night.
    But joy comes with the morning.

The meeting at Tiberius was a joyous morning for the Disciples. The risen Christ, serving them breakfast and moving toward Pentecost.

Our Creator,
you shared with me the food of strength.
I have been able to feed and love, support,
and witness to your love.
I thank you for the wonderful teaching through
Jesus Christ, the Savior.

What About Prayer?

9 Pray then like this:
Our Father who art in heaven,
Hallowed be thy name,
10 Thy kingdom come,
Thy will be done,
    On earth as it is in heaven.
11 Give us this day our daily bread;
12 And forgive us our debts,
    As we also have forgiven our debtors;
13 And led us not into temptation,
    But deliver us from evil.

Matthew 6: 9 – 13

Prayer is the soul's sincere desire uttered or unexpressed. Or *God, give us the grace to accept with serenity the things that cannot be changed, the courage to change the things that should be changed, and the wisdom to distinguish the one from the other.*

Prayer has become a very popular process in this church. And I personally have experienced it once again as in the past because for the third time in my adult life I have placed my trust in a physician to invade my body for three to four hours correcting on this occasion my ability to walk without pain. And it is particularly sobering when the assistant to the surgeon, pulling no punches, states, "We do have some concerns, considering you are 83 going on 84."

One of the greatest concerns is that my sermons be put together with thought, study, and preparation. My concerns that I have always had in the ministry is that I have never been able to pray in public an eloquent prayer. And I often chafe when I am in a meeting, class, church, or secular gathering, and am asked to pray as the professional prayer. In the tradition I was raised in, a priesthood of all believers was the norm. And I grew up in the parsonage and it was often said that when my father prayed at a funeral you almost wished you were the deceased!

Well, let us take an easy way out right now. We all the know the Lord's Prayer, or Prayer of our Father. Let's take a look at it in the light of today.

- It begins by honoring God, Jesus's father, the source of life and creation.
- It includes a supplication for a kingdom, heavenly and according to God's will. (Does today's kingdom measure up?)
- It includes a supplication for bread, the staff of life.
- It asks for forgiveness. No one is perfect and all will make mistakes, but the loving creator offers grace.
- There will be temptations; they are present.
- The source of the kingdom is the God of Love.
- We live under God's power and glory forever.

I have a copy of the recent reprint of the Jefferson Bible. Thomas Jefferson, third President of the newly formed United States, a scholar, statesman, ambassador in his late twenties, believed that the most important value of the New Testament was the sayings of Jesus. Which reminds me that while studying for my doctorate I took a coursed entitled "Sayings of Jesus in the Synoptic Tradition." And as an aside this item appeared on my computer: ". . . what is the value of a Christianity in which Jesus is worshiped as Lord, but Christian discipleship – 'the way of Jesus'—is regarded as largely irrelevant to life in the modern world?"

Jefferson believed it was far more important to know, understand, and follow the teachings of Jesus than to be embroiled in the many doctrines that had accumulated. Even our forefathers believed that primary was the confession of faith, "Jesus is the Christ," and various other doctrines were superfluous.

Now in my own advanced years I agree that too much judgment has been placed on doctrine and not enough on what it means to follow "the way of Jesus." In my years living first as a child in the parsonage and later being aware of my father's ministry, and later in my own ministry, and now ostensibly a layman, I have heard again and again the judgment that the Gospel is not being preached. More likely what is going on is that the criticism comes from a calcification of belief with little forward movement in things spiritual or little growth in faith.

When I was living in Los Angeles and supplying from time to time in churches, one Sunday I was attempting to illustrate the great significance of the Scriptures. I compared the text in Isaiah that says "a young woman shall conceive" to the scripture in Matthew that "a virgin shall conceive." Now any way you wish to read that it is the way it is written. I was trying to tell that the power of God is indeed the power of God and God's revelation was bound to come. A man carrying what I call a ten-pound Bible chastised me at the door, asking if I believed in the virgin birth. I responded by saying the only test of faith I would answer was that I believed that Jesus is the Christ. He promptly cursed me to hell and went flying out the door, his meek, frightened wife following at a respectful distance behind.

Be careful what test you do and also remember a significant admonition: "By what judgment you judge, you shall be judged."

Now I must admit I find myself saying that to myself again and again. Sometimes I allow patience to become thin. After all these years we appear to be in the same place. Thomas Jefferson in the 18th century had greater insight than some of us do now. I have heard it said we need to learn basics and that is what Jefferson wished to write – basics. That does not mean that doctrine has no significance. It is a teaching mechanism meant to explain, to look into the depths of faith, but never to be a test.

Here is another illustration. On my dining room wall I have a triptych I painted of the artist Christo's umbrellas. After he had created the umbrellas, I heard him lecture at Long Beach State. People kept asking him what he was trying or what he meant to say? His answer again and again was "It's art! It's art!" And that is what I believe about the doctrines we hold so dear. They are teaching. They are narrative. Did Jesus talk about his birth, creation, or even the trinity? He talked about what it meant to live the God-revealed life. And he invited his disciples, you and me, to follow him.

So, after all that, let us get to "What about prayer?"

As recorded, the Disciples not only witnessed Jesus at prayer, they heard him pray and finally asked him how to pray. That which we call the Lord's Prayer is then given as an illustration of prayer.

Over the years, and because of experience, my concept of prayer has moved beyond asking for favors. I do not pray for intercession or for miracles. But I do pray to be in contact with the ultimate power in the universe – a soul's sincere desire, seeking the depths of insight and spiritual understanding.

The Lord's Prayer begins in the glorification of the ultimate power and knowledge of the source of life's reality, which we will never know fully, though it is a search we must make. Consider most of all that this is a very Jewish prayer, and as a Jewish prayer it honors the ultimate reality that Jesus refers to as Abba, that is Father, a personal and intimate relationship beyond all others. I have a profound faith in that which we call God. Sometimes I am of the opinion that the name God is too easy and too common. It enters our language in many ways. It is possible that what Jesus used in this prayer is a name considered to be too sacred to be spoken aloud, and Abba is a substitute.

I grew up in a home where prayer and devotion were considered to be a serious matter and never heard in worship the line, "What do you pray about?" Almost like "What's for supper?" Instead there was preparation and quiet entry into that moment. My congregation in Scotland considered what they called "prayers of the church" to be serious, and there were long moments of silence. Now I must admit all this did not come off smoothly at all times. One Sunday an elder got himself so wrapped up in his prayer he did not know how to end it gracefully.

In the Lord's Prayer Jesus begins by speaking of the length, depth, width, and solemnity of the heavenly presence. He taught his disciples that prayer was not a rote formula and that in entering the presence was as great as the presence of Jehovah himself.

In prayer we are not only inviting ourselves into heaven. We are inviting heaven to be present.

It is the next supplication that interests me and makes me humble. We are asking favor, not only asking for a kingdom but the will of the one we honor.

Think about it! Not many months ago we sat in this sanctuary as we have sat for years, extolling the pronouncement: "Peace on earth, good will." Question. Where is it? Two thousand plus years have passed and where is that peace? Is it here? Where is the Kingdom? How much will do we follow in our lives? What is required of us is not that difficult to understand. And what have we done in all these years? We have cluttered up faith with belief in dozens of doctrines ferreted out of another age, other cultures, other prejudices, and made them tests of faith.

In his bible, Thomas Jefferson cut out all the superfluous doctrine and wrote only about the life of Jesus. Now, Jefferson was no saint, and portions of his life can be questioned. But all the same he got to the basics, and it was obvious that he was a profound thinker and concerned about Jehovah's children, the family. Can it be said that in our present circumstances this is what is happening? Are we only concerned with power and the accumulation of wealth? Tell me, how many dollars will it take to establish the Kingdom of God?

Now, I am a realist. What I say here will not make one bit of difference in today's world. But I believe what I say might have some significant appeal regarding our devotional life. And this prayer we pray so easily might disturb the depths of our faith. What we pray here might move beyond asking for favors and go to the depths of our souls as we honor the ultimate reality and seek to be an instrument of peace.

What is next? We pray for bread. Bread – that is a significant core in faith. I don't know how many of you have seen *The Hunger Games*. I have not but I have read the series of books. It is a story of teenagers fighting to acquire food for their particular communities. Of course, there are people of power, mainly adults, urging them on. It is a particularly violent story and surely inspired by the history of the world and the wars for dominance. What's new?

The symbol of bread is important. While I may criticize the idea of asking for favors, there is the idea of the needs of the whole body.

I told Sharon recently that this last 12 months were at times overwhelming. A year ago I had to sit on a stool to bring my message. Even though there are moments of residual pain and problems of balance, much of that is behind me.

Jesus used the distribution of bread on many occasions, such as his feeding of the multitude, breakfast at Tiberius, the appearance at Emmaus, and of course, in The Upper Room. And we sit at the table of the Lord and welcome those who come to the food pantry.

It has been pointed out that in many ways Christianity has a material conscience. In the name of Christ we have built hospitals, clothed those in need, built educational institutions. It is also pointed out that this prayerful supplication to give us our daily bread is in the plural. It says "us." Not me, but us.

There is a frightening philosophy in our nation right now, and moving abroad, and maybe coming from abroad. It is selfish and inward. It is "I have it. I earned it. I keep it." It involves thinking that you have to work as I did, if you want anything. One of the great problems today is the lack of an awareness of the growth of the world, the changes and the intensity of invention and innovation.

Here is an example. For a number of years Sharon's daughter and husband have farmed with success in Washington State. But times have changed and what has been known as "the family farm" is slowly going out of business. And if something happens that makes it difficult physically to farm, just renting it out does not solve the problem or support the family. It was far different over 50 years ago when I was in seminary and preaching in a little town. My church included a number of widows who lived comfortably on their land as it was farmed by renters. The popular mode today is to regress to the past, the sweet past and never to suggest that we must look at progress. Rather than reestablish the past, we must take the energy and vision of the past to improve the world and to proclaim the teaching of Jesus to the least of these.

I have been reading lately the works of a biblical scholar showing the influence of Judaism on Christianity. What is obvious is that Jesus was a Jew and used Jewish ideas in preaching. His motive was to make the authorities in the temple think ahead.

When someone claims to me that a preacher is not preaching the Gospel, he is mainly saying that the preacher has stopped giving him comfort food rather than energy food to work for the future. When some prognosticator writing for a local paper decries the falling off of church attendance, it is because that person has not done his research. I will state the problem. The church, both liberal and evangelical, is still caught in another century, fussing over doctrines that went out with high buttoned shoes. And the church in Rome is so caught up in an archaic theology it does not hear many of its thinkers, particularly the sisters who have been in the forefront of education for years.

Now, let's take the last lines of the Lord's Prayer because they appear together. First they regard forgiveness, then the temptation of evil.

I doubt if one of us has not needed to forgive or be forgiven. It is not easy not to become offended by something. Just watch TV or listen to the radio and you will have seethed at something that has offended you.

A few months ago I traveled to Redondo Beach, California to celebrate the 100th anniversary of a church I pastored for 10 years. I wondered if I would see some of those who gave me a hard time. Interestingly enough, none were there, and I thought how silly of me.

I was taken by an interesting article in *The Christian Century* that came out last month. It told of an association where leaders of various seminaries and colleges meet to hear papers read and discuss mutual concerns of higher education. The gathering is a mix of the left and right, and yet in that setting there is no animosity, but only a fellowship and sharing of concerns.

There is a wrinkle that is sometimes overlooked in the Lord's Prayer. Is there a difference in asking to be forgiven for debts, trespasses, or sins? Not really. But each word does have its own connotation.

What is important, as it is throughout this prayer, is the call for self-examination. How often do we really think about past differences and contemplate that event at Golgotha when Jesus forgave those who were driving nails into his feet and hands?

Finally, there is the last petition or supplication. This is always a difficult one. That is not to be led into temptation, and if falling into temptation, to be quickly dragged out. In some ways it is an admission that we *can* be tempted. We are very human. We must not be so smug that we kid ourselves about being perfect.

Ever come across that person who is so confidently perfect you wonder if he or she ever makes a mistake? Come to think of it I sit behind a woman in art class who is perfect in every way. On occasion she will have a compliment for my work, so she is forgiven even if I wish to ask her, "Do you ever make a mistake?" Of course, I know she does, because she is always making corrections.

Sometimes we are hotwired to yield to temptation. Ever hear of shortcuts or excuses? I was painting the other day and having a difficult time and gave some lame excuse to the instructor, whereupon she shot back at me not to use that excuse because I knew better and had been painting too long not to know better. Right then I had to back into the mode of forgiveness for bringing on myself the deserved criticism.

I am reminded how often the Gospel writers record that Jesus went off by himself to pray. I have wondered and asked if this was his humanity. We have allowed so much of our belief to block out our faith. We have made this Jesus something he did not claim for himself. We have pushed him out to really be unreachable, when in fact he is our personal friend. He said so himself. We should be able to talk with him without being so speechless we cannot be honest. When we hurt we hurt. When we are tempted we are tempted. When we are angry we are angry. When we are pleased and happy, we are happy.

That is why this prayer was taught. It was taught in simple words, plainspoken and true to the core. It is a significant prayer when we say it with meaning and reverence.

Our Creator who is eternal,
praise in your name.
Your world be blessed, your will be our guide,
on earth as it is in eternity.
Give us sustenance to perform our good works.
And forgive us our misadventures
as we forgive the misadventures of others.
Let us not be tempted but strengthened
to do the common good on earth.
For you are the all in all,
the power of truth and the glory forever.

What Does Jesus Do?

27 "But I say to you that hear. Love your enemies, do good to those who hate you.

28 "Bless those who curse you. Pray for those who abuse you."

29 To him who strikes you on the cheek, offer the other also; and from him who takes away your cloak do not withhold your cloak as well.

30 Give to everyone who begs from you; and of him who takes away your goods; do not ask them again.

31 And as you wish that men would do to you, do so to them.

Luke 6: 27–31

The popular question often asked when making a difficult decision, "WHAT WOULD JESUS DO?" In this meditation take that question and ask "WHAT DOES JESUS DO?"

God's truth is one, and though often influenced by custom and tradition, faith does point in one great direction. There is one eternal power and that power is not far off. It is very close and centered in our lives.

Too often in history, and prevalent today, we have turned Jesus into some sort of shaman and called upon him and God to do magic for us, from saving us with a miracle to influencing the outcome of a favorite football team. Granted, we are often thankful for all sorts of good experiences but to believe God's power favors us in some circumstances is ludicrous. Such thinking desensitizes us from the real purpose of Christ. This is the principal expression of God's love for all creation, no exceptions. Jesus is the instrument of relationship to God. We who embrace Christianity as our faith are proclaiming our way to God through the person and work of Jesus Christ. I find in these senior years I am even more reflective on this truth. I believe in a message of relationship with god through the life and ministry of Jesus Christ.

The late and great Disciple of Christ preacher Fred Craddock tells the story of a child who did not know the whole story of her parentage. She loved the church and attending with her mother quietly moving in and out of the service. One week a famous preacher came to preach and she was excited to hear him. When the service was over she attempted to leave unnoticed. As she turned a corner she walked into the preacher's path. He bent down and said, "Whose child are you?" Fear shot through her being. Now everyone, including the preacher, would know her secret. But the preacher answered his question. "You are God's child. Go claim your inheritance!"

That is the message for us all. We are God's children with an immense inheritance. We have an inheritance of God's love and we are taught to channel that love. The announcer of that love is Jesus Christ. It is what he does.

We have a habit of spending much of our time in the trivia of faith, "with mint, anise, and cumin," when before we were born we were loved by God. God is creator, source of our being, our primary relationship-influence in all relationships.

What does Jesus do? We are taught about **compassion**. We are taught about living in love.

Hear those words again: *Do unto others as you would be done by others. Love your enemies, do good to those who hate you, bless those who curse you, give to those in need. This is the commandment: love one another as you have been loved.*

Think of those words as we listen today. Think of then in your own life, as you seek to care for others and give of yourself for others. Compassion answers the question of what does Jesus do? It is central to the teaching of Jesus.

Next to compassion is wisdom, a tremendous word! Job in his search concludes with the question "Where shall wisdom be found?" Job answers his question by reflecting that wisdom was not found in the mountains or the sea, nor in the accumulation of gold. It is found by being able to see God. "*I had heard of thee by the hearing of the ear, but now my eye sees thee.*"

Jesus brings wisdom, he opens truth, he reveals God in life and is the source of wisdom.

Read the story of the prodigal son. It is a story of coming into wisdom. He left home to find his way in the world and ended up feeding pigs. Not a popular occupation for a Jewish boy, but finally, "He came to himself."

Robert Fulghum, author of the book *All I Really Need to Know I Learned in Kindergarten*, holds up the model of a brain and states that in this small melon-sized organ are many of the mysteries of life — a gift, a gift of our creation. It has the capacity to think outside the box, to be creative, to understand many things and to continue to learn well into our senior years.

Fulghum states, "I believe imagination is greater than knowledge. That myth is more potent than history, dreams are more powerful than facts, hope always triumphs over experience, laughter is the only cure for grief and love is stronger than death."

Jesus compares the kingdom with a mustard seed which when planted in the right way can grow into the greatest shrub, a tree, and be filled with all sorts of good things, the leaves, flowers, birds of the air.

And all of this is ready for you and me to discover. Learning what Jesus does opens for us a relationship that is creative, exciting, purposeful.

In a little book entitled *A Credible and Timely Word*, this paragraph appears: "The Gospel has two poles, neither of which may be ignored. If we take the love of God freely offered to us as the only point of the gospel, forgetting the command of God that justice be done to each and all, we will plunge into 'cheap grace." If we take the command of God to do justice to all those whom God loves as the only point while forgetting the empowering and redeeming grace of God, we fall as quickly into works of righteousness." The life and work of Jesus is what we seek.

Compassion and wisdom with knowledge are a never ending journey that reveals more light and truth from The Word. It is not an easy journey, it is a demanding journey. It is a challenge and it is the pathway to our inheritance.

Creator of life,
we are on a journey.
Do not spare us from challenge
and continue to reveal to us the glory of following
Jesus Christ on this journey –
The Way, Truth, and Life.

Life's Distractions

I had heard of thee by the hearing of the ear but now my eye sees thee.

Job 42:5

This is a newer chapter influenced by the recent election. I will not attempt to write in regard to the two parties on the results but to the condition of the country during the election and the division of society and what it is like being a senior citizen.

Most of us, I assume, are pretty much traumatized by the party we have supported all of our adult lives. I know I am. For a short time, I jumped from the party of my family, but only once voted for a candidate other than my family's tradition. Since that time I have pretty much stayed with one party. But that is not the reasons I decided to add this chapter.

This was a particularly brutal campaign and I was disappointed in the candidates' considerable time in character assassination rather than the necessary issues. My concern here is to speak to the issues for those of us who are elderly. As I age I have reflected on the fact that at my age I have accumulated a large amount of experience and considerable reading and study. And of course I have experienced thousands of individuals.

In one of my ministries, I had a mixed congregation of defense personnel, airline pilots, and teachers, including a couple of school principals. Such a variety of persons provided me with a fund of knowledge, an experience more influential to me than reading. And that is why Job 42:5 is a favorite text of mine, but it is about hearing by ear and seeing with eyes. My point is that at an advanced age all of us have a fund of knowledge and experience we need to find a way of sharing.

Sometimes we can be very intrusive! For example, my father was always filled with advice, and it was usually good, but it was important for me to learn how to speak and contribute my own knowledge and experience. In some cultures, the seniors are appreciated and sought for advice, but not so much in ours. Of course, a quick survey of "Dear Abby" or a viewing of "Judge Judy" will give you a different perspective.

As I few older I decided not to have ready answers and formulas but to be available. Of course, children will be interested in hearing of your exploits, experiences, and travel, not necessarily your advice.

There are many talents that come naturally. I have never been much of a cook, but there are recipes and cooking experiences I have learned. And of course my profession and calling as a minister was influenced by my father who schooled me by the protocol of making a pastoral visit, conducting a memorial service, and officiating at a wedding, and most of all, composing and delivering a sermon based on scripture.

All of this is to say that as experience and living our lives we as seniors have a legacy to share life. The full life is not to make sure our paths are followed but to leave a history of our service and most of all pass on our love and admiration to our children and grandchildren. I did not know my grandparents well for they passed away before I was of an age to create a living memory. I had to realize that their legacy to me through my parents and living on that memory. And we who are memoirists need to be aware that this is an important purpose in our senior years. Sometimes what we leave is beyond words and history. I for one took up art, and my children have received art memorabilia of mine. Memory is not always a matter of instruction or wisdom, though that too is important, but often it resides most effectively in a talisman which can be held or treasured and has a history.

Job heard and also visualized. He had heart and his eyes saw the truth in love and he lived it. My eyes see and I see many manifestations of my inheritance and that seeing makes life full.

Though I have had many devotional experiences I have never been one to have a set time for devotions. Yet recently

I discovered that I did. Since the acquisition of a computer, I have found myself most mornings turning on my computer to see the messages and contemplating thoughts and prayers.

When I was a boy I took manual training classes. We made simple things – a box, a toy baseball bat. Only in later years when I was a pastor of a church, participating in volunteer labor, did I realize that early manual training had taught me how to hold a hammer and drive a nail.

Our Creator,
A thanksgiving for the experiences of life,
full of praise and devotion.

Living the Full Life

The LORD is my shepherd
I shall not want;
2 he makes me lie down in green pastures.
He leads me beside still waters;
3 he restores my soul.
He leads me in paths of righteousness
for his name's sake.

4 Even though I walk through the valley of the shadow
    of death,
I fear no evil;
for thou art with me;
thy rod and thy staff,
they comfort me.

5 Thou preparest a table before me
in the presence of my enemies;
Thou anointest my head with oil,
my cup overflows.
Surely goodness and mercy shall follow me
all the days of my life;
and I shall dwell in the house of the LORD
for ever.

                                                    Psalm 23

I must confess I put off for a long time finishing this book
with a closing chapter. But one morning I woke up and I have
this habit of often going over ideas for sermons as I contemplate
my day. I do it now on occasion, even though I have a long time
been retired. And it occurred to me, what is the most familiar
poetic scripture in the Bible? The 23rd Psalm of course.

Back about 1958 when the Disciples of Christ sent me to Scotland to pastor a church, my family and I were met at our ship and transported from Glasgow, across Scotland, to a town on the Firth of Forth, Kirkcaldy. We arrived after this six day voyage on the Empress of Britain having experienced on the Atlantic a force eight gale. We were not really ready to "make nice" with a group of people speaking a dialect different from our own. The house – we were told it would be "the manse" or parsonage – was full of people, members of the oversight committee or official board. They treated us with kindness. We first went about the practice of placing our two young children, very tired, to bed. Not all that easy in a new house, new experience, and also a new was of speaking "other than American."

Finally the gathering adjourned to the living room. Introductions plus devotions were presented and we heard the 23rd Psalm sung to the tune of Jessie Seymour Irvine's "Crimond." It was beautiful and it set the beginning of a three year ministry to a congregation of people with a long tradition in the history of the denomination in which I was raised and educated. I know I speak of that ministry too often but at this age it is one of those experiences and devotions that never diminish.

And so it is in this Psalm. It is filled with promise and as we move through our years we begin to realize that again and again we have been nourished at the table and have moved through adversity with strength and support. We have indeed lived a full life no matter the number of years we have enjoyed. One time during my years as a local pastor I was looking around the children's classroom in the education department. And it appeared the children were creating drawings of various scriptures, one being the 23rd Psalm. One of the drawings depicted a child walking along a path and behind the child were two little figures following with the titles "Goodness and Mercy." I could not but hope that idea stayed with that child.

I have always wondered why we in American don't sing the 23rd Psalm to "Crimond." This great Psalm and hymn often runs through my head as I prepared my day and particularly my sermons and devotions.

Be aware! It is filled with promise, the promises of the life laid out for us not only in the whole story of the scriptures but particularly in the life of Jesus Christ.

I cannot help but end with this thought. I often read about some person, usually a celebrity of some sort who has "found Jesus." Found Jesus? You have found Jesus? No, Jesus found you and claimed you from the beginning. What needs to happen is your awakening – growing and knowing Jesus.

Jesus like a shepherd lead me.

So many challenges in life –
Some are good and many are difficult
particularly late in life.
You are my shepherd.

In these pages I offer my prayers.
I pray for my faith,
rejoicing for this time
of dedication and opportunity
to express my joys and concerns.

I pray for the family of my church.
It meets the needs of so many people.
It takes pleasure in faith and joy
For those who are near and far.

Blessed are those who minister to us.
They continue in their dedication,
teaching us in a spiritual way of life.

And most of all I write
on these pages my meditations
and pray fervently
that the peace of understanding
be lived throughout the world.

Resources

There are many resources that have influenced me, most notably the Bible, both the RSV and NRSV. Writing as I have here, footnoting every reference would surely be tedious to the reader. Here then is a kind of combination bibliography and acknowledgment.

Sharon B. Jarman, M.A., my wife.

Rev. Dr. Ray C. Jarman. From the beginning of my life I was the recipient of his sermons and his wisdom.

Rev. Dr. Larry Snow, my present pastor. We have had many discussions regarding aging.

Rev. Dr. David Arnold, my friend and supporter.

Rev. Dr. John Cobb. One of my professors at the Claremont School of Theology.

Donald Clingan, "Aging Persons in the Community of Faith."

John Shelby Spong, *The Sins of Scripture.*

Marcus J. Borg & John Dominic Crossan, books and lectures.

Karen Armstrong, *History of God.*

Art Morgan, *Art Morgan Blue Sheet*

Will M. Clements, *Ministry with the Aging.*

Diane Butler Bass, *A People's History of Christianity.*

Henri J. M. Nouwen, *The Return of the Prodigal Son.*

Linel Corbbett and Michael Carbine, editors, *Jung and Aging.*

Mary Pipher, *Another Country.*

Harold R. Nelson, *Senior Spirituality.*

Seward Hiltner, *Toward a Theology of Aging.*

Brian D. McLaren, *A New Kind of Christianity.*

Zalman Schachter-Shalomi and Ronald S. Miller, *Aging to Sage-ing.*

Mark Jarman, *Bone Fires: New and Selected Poems*.

Robert McDowell, The Poetry Mentor.

Fred Craddock, *Preaching*.

Barbara Wingate, M.S.W., pamphlet, "If the Trolley's in Sight: A Practical Legal and Financial Guide for People with Life-threatening Illnesses"